Presentation by *BookLeaf Publishing*

Web: www.bookleafpub.com

E-mail: info@bookleafpub.com

ISBN: 9789395620932

First edition 2022

Dear Miss, I wish you knew.

Majella Ritchie

DEDICATION

To my young people. This is dedicated to you. You continue to amaze me with your strength and perseverance. Thank you for allowing me to be part of your journey and teaching me so much about life. Your words are with me everywhere I go. I hope you know that no matter where you are in life I will always be proud of you.

ACKNOWLEDGEMENT

I would like to acknowledge the Aboriginal and Torres Strait Islander peoples of Australia and pay my respects to my elders past, present and emerging. I would like to honour the First Nations Children that I have had the pleasure of teaching and learning from. May we pave a pathway that is committed to healing, reconciliation and a better tomorrow for our future generations.

PREFACE

Every day, my young people say something that touches me. Whether it is a funny joke, a shocking truth or words of wisdom, every conversation is truly special. I want to hold onto these words and allow these words to touch other people's lives and allow them to understand the lives that our marginalised experience. These poems are a reminder to never judge someone unless you have walked a mile in their shoes.

Why I can't call Mum

Dear Miss,

I wish you knew this
I stopped calling my mother
she said I bring shame to her and my brother
I long to hear her voice
but right now, this is my choice
you are the one I look to
please help me because I don't have a clue
I can't ask anyone for help
though it's the thing I need to yelp
I will not look weak
even though my future is bleak
please know when I say I am fine
I am really wishing for what is mine
a hug from my mum
or my brother to call me dumb
instead I look at the silent phone
and hope to one day go home

Please don't give up on me Miss

Dear Miss,

I wish you knew
the days are getting harder to get through
I want to change
These feelings emerging in me are strange
You tell me violence is bad
but it's all I learned from my dad
I wanted you so badly to be proud of me
but all I know is fight or flee
Please Miss, don't give up on me just yet
I really don't want to come across as a threat
Your words help me every single day
I thank the Lord as I pray
I will not end up like him
even though the light may be dim
I know I can do this
Please don't give up on me Miss

Happy Birthday Miss!

Dear Miss,

Today is your birthday
The boys and I spent all week planning for this
day
I know we don't have much to give
but we hope we make today a memory for you
to relive
You make our days better
So for your birthday we wrote you a letter
to say thank you for everything
especially the kindness you bring
you look at us with belief
with you there's no thought of grief
So Miss here is to celebrating you
A person who is so true.

The nights make me blue

Dear Miss

I wish you knew how hard the nights are
I saw goodbye to you at the end of each day
You get in your car
and so easily drive away
but my day stays the same
no change in sight
I am surrounded by the same four walls
every hour is a constant fight
I listen to the outside through meaningless phone
calls
Miss, your voice is what gets me through
our chats about life
teaching me is what you do
telling me to stay out of strife
around you I put on a smile
but little do you know I scream through the night
it only lasts for a while
But Miss, I hope you're right
when you say things will get better
But Miss, I wish you knew
maybe I should write it to you in a letter
but the nights sure make me blue.

Finding out my fate

Dear Miss,

Today I find out my fate
It's the dreaded day I await
You are trying to keep me occupied
So I will put my stresses aside
I know you know what today is means
finding out if I am forever locked up in my teens
You tell me no matter what it will be okay
once I get through this dreaded day
I know how society looks at me
They think I should not be free
The guard calls out my name
I put my head down in shame
You take my hand and tell me it will be alright
My chest is pounding and tight
Tears burning in my eyes
As 'good luck' is called out by the guys
I turned around and see your face
Knowing your belief in me is my saving grace.

The colour of my skin

Dear Miss

I wish you knew what happens when I walk the
streets
every man and child sees me and retreats
they see the colour of my skin
and the discrimination starts to begin
a woman sees me and starts running away
you see this happens to me every day
it's like being black is wrong
this racism has gone on for way too long
You tell me that I can change society
but the colour of my skin causes me anxiety
why do they see us and run
it's always our people who are faced with the
undone
Miss, I wish everyone could see us the way you
do
Maybe then people would see us in good view

My first award

Dear Miss

I wish you knew what today meant to me
you presented me with my education degree
to achieve this while locked away
is not something I thought would happen on any
given day
you told everyone at the ceremony that I was a
pleasure to teach
I felt taken aback by your speech
you said I am a student who changed your life
but in the mirror all I see is someone who causes
strife
this is my first award I have received
and it's because you believed
I am more than just a troubled man
I am now someone with a life plan
Miss you are my favourite teacher
My qualification is now by best feature.

Bye Mum

Dear Miss,

I wish you knew what I felt last night
My mum went into the light
I didn't get to say goodbye
but I know she's flying high
I don't understand why she had to go
crying is not something I can show
I miss her so much
Just one last hug or even a touch
I think it's my fault for being locked away
maybe this is the price I have to pay
I have never felt so alone
I won't even get to see her grave stone
Miss, I'm sorry I can't get much work done today
Just please tell me that it's going to be okay.

Fly High Brother

Dear Miss,

I wish you knew I'd never seen you cry
until today when you told us our brother has
gone to fly high
I know how much he meant to you
this is not something any of us should go
through
it made me realise just how much you care
but maybe I never made myself aware
that we aren't just an inmate
though I'm sure society would debate
we are someone you truly care for
maybe other school kids deserve you more
but today we lost a friend
and Miss on you I know I can depend
that we will all get through this for sure
so fly high my brother forever more
I will never stop wiping the tears away
because you aren't here to stay.

My son

Dear Miss,

I wish you knew that last night I had a son
I think creating him is the best thing I have done
I couldn't be at his birth
Missing out on this was the worst thing on earth
I cried as he had his first cry
I promised him I will change and really try
Thank you Miss for encouraging me to be a
good dad
You've been teaching me how to read which is
something I am glad
I can't wait to read a book to my boy
Who knew reading is something I would enjoy
I can't wait to hold him tight
for the first time in my life I feel like things
might be alright
So please Miss keep teaching me
So for my son I can be the best I can be.

I'm sorry Miss

Dear Miss,

I wish you knew I hated seeing you look like
that at me
Being a failure is all I can see
I promised you I wouldn't be back
but in the moment all I saw was black
I know I have done wrong
I haven't even been out for that long
You tell me you're happy I am safe and sound
but the truth is I wish I was below ground
You don't know what happens on the outside
I told you I'm sorry and you replied
We just try again okay?
This is not something I thought you would say
But you look at me and smile
knowing I will be in here for a while
But Miss I knew coming back in
was my only chance at trying again.

Don't look Miss

Dear Miss,

I wish you knew why my wrist look like this
It's the only thing that takes the pain away
but the feelings come back each day
I asked you for help in class today
but numbers is not the help I wish to say
I see your eyes move to my arm
your face quickly hides any alarm
you look at me and say
I'm really glad you came to class today
I know you meant every word
I smile and promise to remember what I heard
to hear someone is glad I am here
takes away a tiny bit of fear
that I am worthy of being alive
Thank you Miss for helping me survive.

I am scared Miss

Dear Miss,

I wish you knew how nervous I feel
being so close to my freedom just doesn't seem
real
what if I freak out
what if I start to doubt
that I can't make it outside these walls of
concrete
I feel so incomplete
You tell me you are so happy to hear of the news
I want to be a winner but what if I lose
What if I can't work out how to use the new
iphone
the world of technology is all unknown
I want to tell you I'm scared
I really don't feel prepared
you tell me to take one step at a time
and forget the life of crime
and become what I've always wanted to be
which is to live young and free
I say goodbye to you
you go on about how much I grew
but really all I can think
is how to say no to drugs and a drink

but I know I have to try
because I have to leave the past behind and say
goodbye.

Merry Christmas Miss

Dear Miss,

I wish you knew how much I hated Christmas
Day
I just hope it goes fast and fades away
you are so excited for this day to come
all I can tell you is not seeing my family makes
me numb
You decorate this place
to make it a happier and festive place
I don't know why you want to make it special for
us
maybe this is something we can discuss
but I know seeing all of this red and green
makes me forget I am locked up at eighteen
you tell me Santa comes tonight
I try not to laugh as I stare at you in sight
and tell you he's not real
you say you believe what you feel
I wake the next day with a present to my name
you look at me and say I bet Santa came
So Merry Christmas Miss
I guess this year Christmas was a little bliss.

I can use my words

Dear Miss,

I wish you knew how hard it is to not fight
you tell me using my words is what is right
there's a fella here I can't stand
everything within me wants to use a fist and a
hand
but you pull me aside
so I can openly confide
and tell me to use my voice
forget the violence it's not a choice
I tell you it's the only way to solve things here
but for some reason you get in my ear
and tell me about conflict resolution
fighting does not bring retribution
I say I'll try your way and use my words
I explain to the fella my conditions and terms
we talk things out
there's no fighting about
I realise this feels good
to talk and feel understood
So Miss I guess you are right
violence is not alright
using my words is the way to resolve
who would've thought that I would ever evolve.

Miss I don't know the cultural way

Dear Miss,

I wish you knew that my culture brings me
shame
It's become something I cannot claim
People use it against me
because of this I can't be who I want to be
you see my grandmother got taken away
they did the same thing to me in last year in May
I wonder if it would be different if I was white
Maybe then it would be safe to walk at night
I long to learn of cultural ways
but right now it's just a haze
my family is suffering from the hurt and sorrow
my younger brother holds on for a better
tomorrow
but Miss I really don't know who I am
I don't think this nation gives Aboriginality a
damn
so I'm sorry when I say
I really don't understand the cultural way.

Miss can you please plait my hair?

Dear Miss,

I wish you knew how much I love when you
plait my hair
there's not feeling in the world that can compare
it reminds me of when I was a little girl
my Mum would put my hair in a twirl
I don't really remember much of Mum
I was taken away when I was still sucking my
thumb
how funny we both ended up in chains
maybe it runs through our veins
but when you fix my hair all nice
it makes me forget that I'm paying a price
it makes me feel closer to my mother
I hope one day I can tell her I love her.

Miss I am ready to learn

Dear Miss,

I wish you knew I set up my room last night
having my own bed is quite alright
you see I normally sleep on a park bench
eventually you get used to the stench
Winter is when it gets tough
fighting for a warm place to sleep is tough
but in here I get my own bed
warm blankets and I'm even fed!
So Miss I am here ready to learn
because last night my sleep was not a concern.

Miss I want to be a hairdresser

Dear Miss

I wish you knew I can't see past sixteen
everyone gets excited about turning eighteen
it's just not something I envision
I don't believe living is my decision
you ask me what dream job would be
the truth is no one in my family has had a job or
degree
you tell me to think about it
this was a harder task than I'll admit
being a hairdresser might be a good career
you say let's do it while you're here
I learn from you that dreams can be hard to
achieve
you tell me it's okay because you believe
that I can do anything I set my mind too
including over coming what life has put me
through
so I start to believe that may sixteen isn't where
my life will end
maybe my future can continue to extend.

Miss I hate my birthday

Dear Miss

I wish you knew how much I hated my birthday
It's just a day I wish would go away
You ask me if I'm excited for it
I tell you not even one single bit
You hang up a banner and I have a cake
Celebrating me is just not something I can take
I never had anyone make me feel special before
I was a child my family wished to ignore
but not this year you say
I half smile and say okay
everyone around me starts to sing
It's such an unusual thing
but maybe today wasn't so bad
so Miss I'm sorry I got so mad
but I really do hate my birthday
but this year you made it okay.

Why do you work here Miss?

Dear Miss,

I always wonder why do you work here
It's not the usual teaching career
You friends and family must think you're a fool
do you miss teaching in a normal school?
do you tell everyone all the happiness and jokes
we make?
do you tell them we are kids who made a
mistake?
tell them we love going to Maths and English
with you
you are what gets us through
I bet everyone thinks this is a scary place to be
Miss I really hope you don't agree
but I do wonder why you work in this place
Please know you are someone we could never
replace.

www.ingramcontent.com/pod-product-compliance
Lightning Source LLC
Chambersburg PA
CBHW061324140726
47998CB00007B/2545